SPOTLIGHT ON THE RISE OF MODERN CHINA

Alan Blackwood

Wayland

SPOTLIGHT ON HISTORY

Spotlight on the Age of Exploration and Discovery
Spotlight on the Age of Revolution
Spotlight on the Agricultural Revolution
Spotlight on the Cold War
Spotlight on the Collapse of Empires
Spotlight on Elizabethan England
Spotlight on the English Civil War
Spotlight on the First World War
Spotlight on the Industrial Revolution
Spotlight on Industry in the Twentieth Century
Spotlight on Medieval Europe
Spotlight on Post-War Europe
Spotligt on the Reformation
Spotlight on Renaissance Europe
Spotlight on the Rise of Modern China
Spotlight on the Russian Revolution
Spotlight on the Second World War
Spotlight on the Victorians

Cover illustration: A poster advertising consumer goods in Peking today.

First published in 1986 by Wayland (Publishers) Ltd.
61 Western Road, Hove, East Sussex BN3 1JD, England

British Library Cataloguing in Publication Data
Blackwood, Alan
Spotlight on the Rise of Modern China.—
(Spotlight on History)
1. China—History
I. Title II. Series 951 DS735

ISBN 0-85078-667-3

Printed in Great Britain at The Bath Press, Avon

CONTENTS

1 THE MIDDLE KINGDOM

The Great Wall of China is the only man-made object on our planet large enough to be visible from outer space. This amazing 2,000-year-old structure, which runs for thousands of kilometres across some of the most rugged country in the world, is also a memorial to the longest-lasting civilization in history.

The early civilizations of India, the Middle East and Egypt may be slightly older—dating back to some time before 3,000 BC. But they all died out and were replaced by others, which in their turn flourished and declined. Our own European or Western culture, based largely on the civilizations of Greece and Rome, began about 1,000 years ago, in what historians call the Early Middle Ages.

The Great Wall of China—one of the greatest achievements of Chinese civilization.

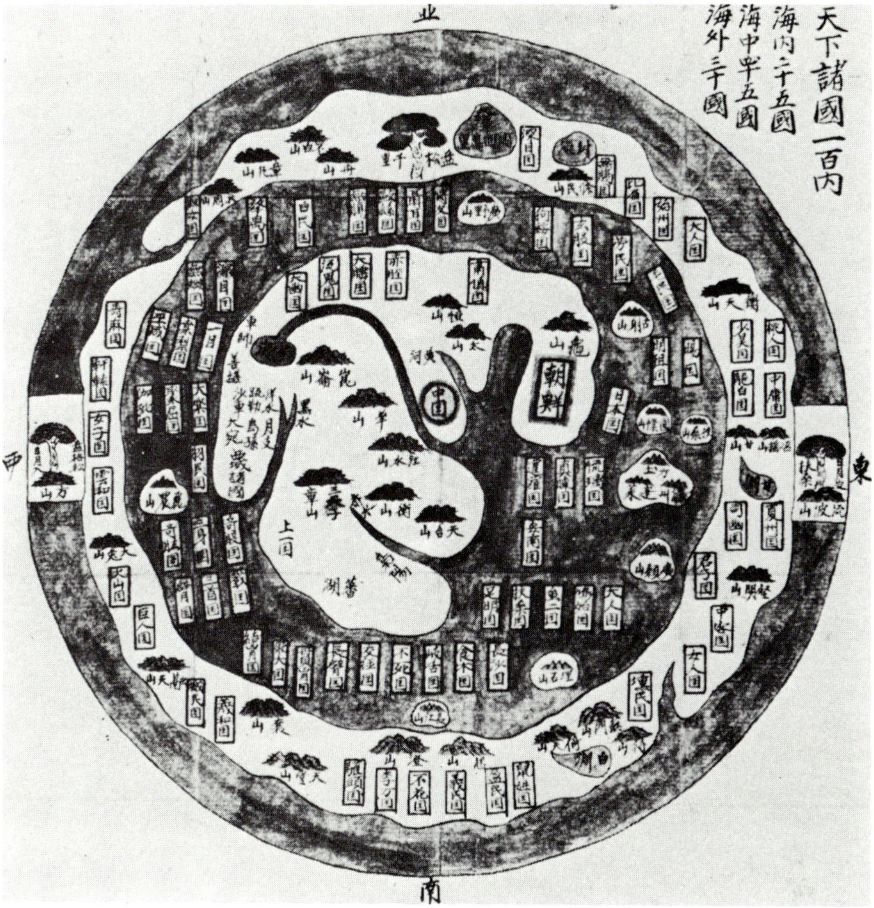

An ancient map of the world, showing China at the centre of the Earth, which was where the Chinese believed their country to be.

The history of China, by contrast, is an almost continuous record of one civilization over a period of 3,000 years. It is as though we in the West could trace our own language and religion, literature, music and painting, science and law, directly back to the time of the pyramids; and as though, until very recently, we had still been ruled by a pharoah.

Giant of the East

The Chinese people used to call their land 'The Middle Kingdom', believing that it occupied the very middle or centre of the earth. On their maps it took up nearly all the area shown, being surrounded on its fringes by the islands of Japan, the mountains of the Himalayas, India, and right over on the extreme edge, a small part of Africa and

A crowd at a political meeting in Peking. One quarter of the world's population is Chinese.

Europe. To a people whose own land was so large, and who knew of nowhere else that could begin to match their own level of culture and civilization, such a view of the world was perfectly reasonable.

China, though only a part of Asia, is as large as some continents. Its land area of 9,560,940 sq km (3,691,500 sq miles) is almost equal to that of the whole of Europe. It has a 4,000 km (2,500 mile) coastline bordering on the Pacific Ocean. Its vast interior encompasses Tibet and most of the Himalayas, with Mount Everest itself marking the frontier with Nepal. It is a land of tremendous contrasts of climate and landscape, ranging from tropical monsoons to near-Arctic cold, and from scenes of exquisite natural beauty to trackless desert.

The superlatives do not end there. China heads the population league with 1,000 million citizens, one quarter of the world total. The cities of Peking (the capital) and Shanghai (the biggest sea port) each have populations of over eight million, though the majority of people still live in the countryside, especially in the region of the two longest rivers, the Yangtze and Huang Ho (or Yellow River).

Chinese civilization

The Chinese were probably the first people to invent paper and printing, gunpowder and rockets. And yet, until this century, they remained a backward nation in terms of industry and technology. The size of China and the fact that it was self-contained, and run for so many centuries by a scholarly civil service, created a mood of complacency. New inventions and ideas were often overlooked, and the spirit of enterprise was stifled.

Confucius, the Chinese philosopher and teacher, who lived from 551–478 BC.

Despite such shortcomings, in nearly every field of endeavour Chinese civilization has a marvellous record. From its earliest period, Chinese craftsmen led the world in the use of bronze and other metals, in ceramics (notably in the manufacture of the finest porcelain bowls and jars, cups and saucers), and in the carving of wood, ivory and jade (a type of stone that has had a special attraction for the Chinese).

Chinese thought and wisdom are enshrined in the names of Confucius (Kung Fu Tzu), who lived 500 years before Christ, and the legendary Lao Tze, founder of the religion or philosophy of Taoism in the sixth

Animals and plants are vividly portrayed in this twelfth-century Chinese painting. In the foreground a small figure is playing a flute.

century BC. Their ideas—respect for authority, living in peace and harmony with nature—have profoundly influenced Chinese painting and design, which is admired for its refinement, calm and order.

In the fields of science and medicine, Chinese astronomers produced the oldest known celestial maps or star charts, and by observations of the sun, calculated the length of the year to within twenty seconds. Acupuncture, their ancient method of healing, has recently attracted much interest in the West. This shares Taoist ideas about harmony, and seeks to correct the balance of energies in a sick person's body.

Chinese poetry, drama and music have an equally rich and illustrious past, but are not so much appreciated outside China itself. This is due to the problems of language and Western unfamiliarity with Chinese systems of musical scales.

The dynasties

The main periods of Chinese history are named after dynasties—successions of kings or emperors belonging to a particular royal family or similar ruling group. A full list of these would be quite long and complicated, because there were times when China was divided between different rulers. The principal dynasties were as follows: Shang (1650–1122 BC), Chou (1122–255 BC), Han (206 BC–AD 220), Tang (618–906), Sung (960–1279), Yuan (1279–1368), Ming (1368–1644) and finally Manchu (1644–1912).

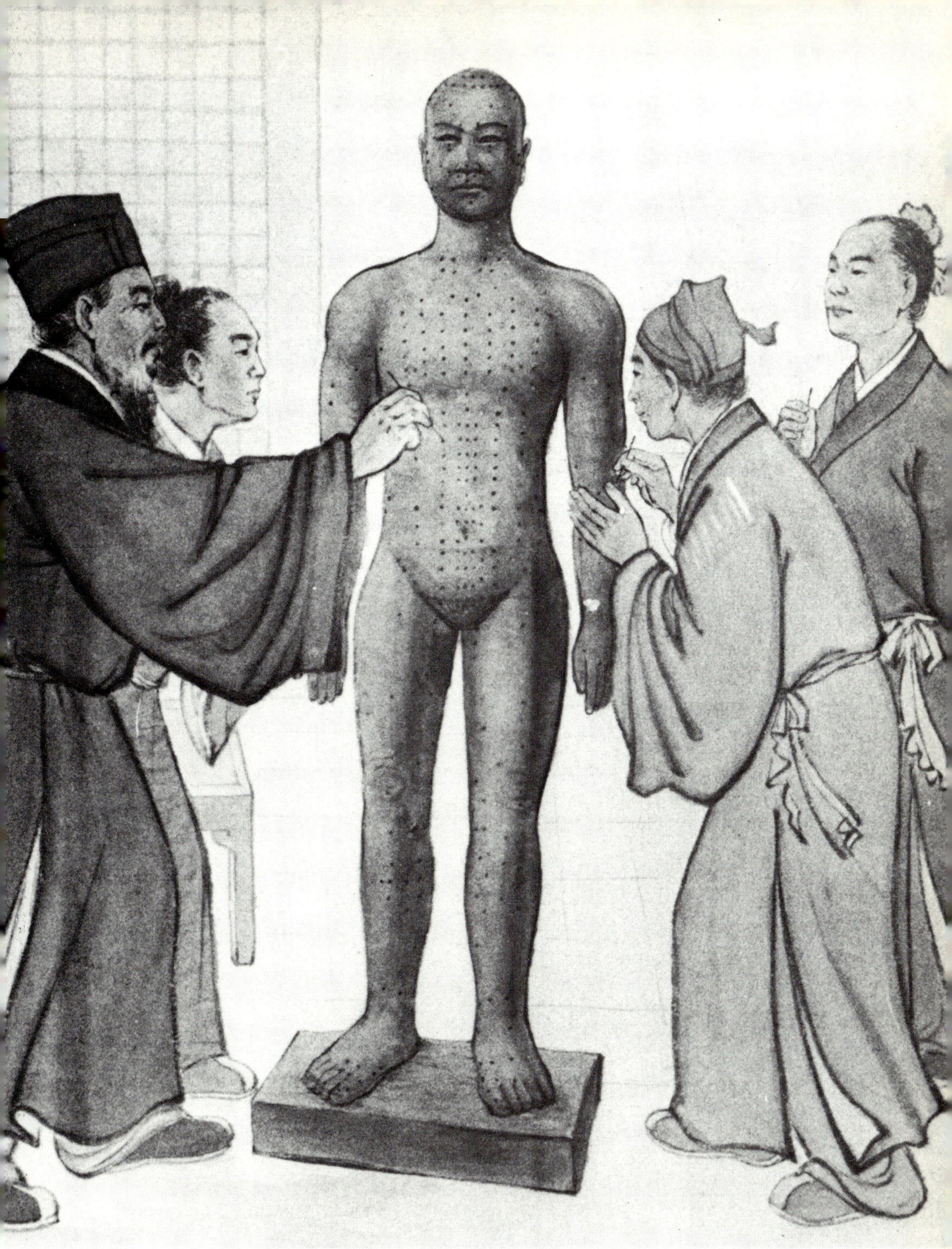

An old illustration showing students learning acupuncture, using a larger than life-size model of the human body.

Chinese pottery has always been highly prized. This 400-year-old dish portrays the five-toed Imperial Chinese dragon.

Some of these names are well known in the West, because they are associated with artistic achievements. Ming, for example, describes a particularly fine type of porcelain. The emperors themselves, like monarchs anywhere, were a mixed bunch, some good, some very bad. A few stand out from the rest.

Most famous is the thirteenth-century Mongol emperor Kublai Khan, founder of the short-lived Yuan dynasty, whose court was so vividly described by the explorer Marco Polo. Another, far more ancient emperor was recently in the news when archaeologists discovered a whole army of life-size earthenware soldiers and horsemen guarding his tomb. This was Shih Huan Ti, the first ruler of a fully unified China, who became Emperor in 221 BC. It was he who began work on the Great Wall, to defend China against invaders. He was, apparently, also a very hard and ruthless man—a reminder that China, for all its splendours, has known as much cruelty and bloodshed as any other civilization.

2 THE SLEEPING GIANT

'On this day the Great Khan receives gifts of more than 100,000 white horses. And on this day also there is a procession of elephants, fully 5,000 in number, all draped in fine clothes embroidered with beasts and birds. Each one bears on its back two strong-boxes of great beauty and price, filled with the Khan's plate and with costly apparel. With them come innumerable camels also draped with cloths and laden with provisions for the feast. They all defile in front of the Great Khan and it is the most splendid sight that was ever seen.'

So wrote Marco Polo of the New Year celebrations at the court of the Emperor Kublai Khan. Marco Polo, a thirteenth-century

One of the first encounters between East and West: the Emperor Kublai Khan (seated) receives Marco Polo and a companion at his court.

A busy Chinese trading post with foreign merchants landing goods. Greedy European traders saw China only as a source of wealth.

Venetian merchant, was one of the first Europeans to reach China and see something of its wonders. There were times when China advanced beyond its frontiers—when it attacked its enemies, or when Chinese merchants sailed the high seas in search of trade. But for much of its long history China was enclosed and secretive, too much involved in internal affairs to bother with the outside world. This was what made it such a mysterious and fascinating place to foreigners. After Marco Polo, more and more Europeans headed east for the strange and exotic land they called Cathay.

Missionaries and merchants

Some of the first Europeans to follow Marco Polo to China, were Christian missionary priests. This was a honeymoon period in Sino-European relations. The missionaries, generally treated by their hosts with tolerant amusement, nonetheless introduced European knowledge and ideas to them.

However, relations deteriorated when it came to trade. By the middle of the sixteenth century, traders from many parts of Europe were converging on the East. The British East India Company, and other trading concerns, viewed China as a 'Sleeping Giant'—a land full of riches, such as silk and tea, there for the taking. The Chinese, on their part, resented the Portuguese, Dutch, British and French merchantmen who entered Canton and other big ports in ever increasing numbers. They did not need to trade, and regarded the foreigners as money-grubbing intruders.

The opium wars

Things came to a head during the nineteenth century—the age of European, and especially British, imperialism. The prime cause of the trouble was opium, to which millions of Chinese were addicted. The British produced the drug in India and shipped it to China at great profit.

Opium smokers in a nineteenth-century Chinese opium den. British exploitation of the drug trade led to war between China and Britain.

European ships bombarding Canton Harbour in 1840, during the Opium Wars.

As one British official cynically put it, 'If the Chinese must be poisoned by opium, I would rather they were poisoned for our benefit than for the benefit of any other exchequer.'

The Chinese themselves at first tried to reason with Britain. Their trade commissioner wrote a letter to Queen Victoria. 'Is there any single article from China which has done any harm to foreign countries? There is, however, a class of treacherous barbarians who manufacture opium, smuggle it for sale, and deceive our foolish people in order to injure their bodies and derive profit therefrom. Such behaviour is repugnant to the feelings of human beings, and is not tolerated by the ways of God. I now propose that we shall unite to put a final stop to this curse of opium. On receipt of this letter make haste to reply, stating the measures which have been adopted at all seaports for cutting off the supply.'

Such entreaties having no effect, in 1839 the Chinese authorities confiscated a large consignment of opium and expelled British traders. In a classic exercise of 'gunboat diplomacy', British warships retaliated by bombarding Canton, Shanghai and other ports, and sailed up the Yangtze to destroy a part of Nanking. The Chinese were forced to submit. Britain claimed Hong Kong as a crown colony and allowed the lucrative drug traffic to continue. France, the United States and other Western powers also demanded special and advantageous trading rights with China.

The Taiping and Boxer rebellions

The Chinese people rebelled, both against the 'foreign devils' and against their own apparently weak and impotent Manchu Government. The Taiping (Heavenly Kingdom) Rebellion of 1850–64 was inspired by a Christian movement within China, dedicated to overthrowing the corrupt and ungodly Manchu regime. Britain, France and other

British troops attacking Taiping cavalry near Peking in 1860, during the Taiping rebellion.

so-called 'Christian' nations, however, saw the morally upright Taiping movement as a new threat to their own dubious trading rights, and sent a military force to back the Manchus. It was led by an army officer whose exploits made him a popular British hero, General 'Chinese' Gordon (killed many years later in the Sudan).

He advised the Manchus on how to put down the Taipings. There was another attack on Nanking, one of the Taiping strongholds. 'Smoke and flame from the burning buildings filled the air,' reported a Manchu agent to his government. 'We searched the city and in three days killed over 100,000 men.' After another massacre of Taiping supporters, an English visitor described the ground as 'literally white like snow with skulls and bones.' An estimated 20 million Chinese were slaughtered before the uprising was suppressed. Another casualty was the beautiful Summer Palace outside Peking, which British and French troops sacked and then razed to the ground.

Taiping supporters lying dead in one of their forts after its capture in August 1860.

The Boxer rebellion was an attempt by some Chinese to eradicate foreign influence in China. Here, Boxer rebels are being taken prisoner.

China's troubles were far from over. As the result of a short but disastrous war with Japan (in 1894–95), she lost Korea and Formosa. Then, in 1900, the Russians, moving in from Siberia, grabbed part of China's northern coastline as an outlet to the Pacific.

All this sparked off another rebellion in 1900—the Boxer Uprising—so named because its ringleaders called themselves The Society of Righteous and Harmonious Fists, and practised a type of ritual boxing. For a few months the fanatical Boxers ran riot, seeking out and murdering not only foreigners but any of their fellow-countrymen who were Christians, or in any other way tainted by foreign contact. Their reign of terror was put down by another international force (this time including troops from the new German Empire), and China was presented with more humiliating terms. It really looked as though the 'Giant' was bleeding to death.

3 BIRTH OF THE REPUBLIC

The Manchu Government was largely responsible for China's wretched state. The first Manchu emperors had ruled well, but like any ruling group in power for too long, their regime had become decadent and corrupt. At the beginning of the twentieth century China was ruled by the Empress Tzu Hsi, who had come to power as a concubine or mistress of the reigning emperor. Vanity ruled her life. 'I have often thought that I am the cleverest woman who ever lived,' she said,

The Empress Tzu Hsi with some of the ladies of her court, photographed in 1903.

Hsuan Tung, the last emperor of China. When the revolution began, the six-year-old emperor abdicated.

as her country's plight grew worse almost by the hour. 'Although I have heard much of Queen Victoria, I don't think her life is half as interesting and eventful as mine.' She promised, among many other things, to give China a modern navy. The nearest she got to it was the building of a lake-side pavilion of pure marble, designed like a pleasure boat, for her tea parties.

Surprisingly, the Empress Tzu Hsi was not assassinated or deposed. She died in 1908, by which time the situation in China was very bad. She was replaced by Hsuan Tung—a young child who was to be China's last emperor. When the inevitable revolution came, in 1912, the six-year-old emperor abdicated.

One of the founders of modern China, Dr Sun Yat Sen, seen here in 1896, the year of his dramatic kidnap in London.

Sun Yat Sen

Foreign intervention in China's affairs, as bad as it was, brought with it some hopeful developments. New industry came to China, and new political ideas were circulated. Chinese people also began to travel and study abroad, something they could not have done at almost any time in the past.

Dr Sun Yat Sen was one of those who went abroad, and, during the 1890s, he studied medicine in Britain, the United States and Japan. His travels also aroused his interest in politics. As matters went from bad to worse in China, he joined and then led a political group called the Revolutionary League. It was founded on 'Three People's Principles': Nationalism, the freeing of China from foreign control; Democracy, the creation of a form of government based on free elections; and the People's Livelihood, the redistribution of land so that each peasant household could support itself.

Sun's activities soon got him into trouble, and he had to flee the country. In 1896 he was living in exile in London, seeking support for his League among the local Chinese, when, in circumstances worthy of a spy thriller, he was kidnapped by Manchu agents and locked up in the Chinese embassy. With the aid of an English friend he escaped, just before he was due to be smuggled out of England and shipped back to China for torture and execution.

He was in London again, in 1911, when news reached him that revolution had at last broken out in China. He hurried home, where he was invited to become the Provisional President of the First Chinese Republic.

Sun Yat Sen (front row, centre) at the formation of the Chinese Revolutionary League.

Yuan Shih Kai became President of the Chinese Republic, but betrayed his promises to the people and was assassinated in 1916.

Hope and despair

The Manchus had gone, but there was still tough resistance to change from China's privileged and powerful ruling classes. The greatest opposition came from the so-called 'war lords', the old military caste, headed by Marshal Yuan Shih Kai. While Sun and his colleagues were trying to create a democratic form of government in Nanking, Yuan threatened a military take-over from the imperial capital of Peking. To try and save his country from civil war, Sun agreed to resign in favour of Yuan, when the latter promised to uphold the principles of the new republic.

Yuan's promises were worthless. Once in power, he behaved just like a Manchu emperor, seeking foreign aid to back him up, quickly dismantling the republic and re-establishing a police state. A feeling of hopelessness and despair once more swept the nation. 'The Revolution of 1911 had indeed brought a ray of light to the age-long darkness', wrote one of Sun's followers. 'It brought joy and encouragement to the people, but in a short time, Yuan Shih Kai usurped state power, and threw the whole nation into a dark abyss again. The people's despair was so great they could hardly bear it, and many committed suicide.'

The new protagonists

Yuan was assassinated in 1916, whereupon Sun and the supporters of his new Nationalist (Kuomintang) Party struggled once more to bring order and peace to their unhappy country. After several more years of near anarchy, they succeeded in organizing free elections, and in 1924, China's first National Congress assembled in Canton, with the Kuomintang as the majority party and Sun as President for the second time.

Alas for China, Sun died the next year, leaving the political arena to the two men who, for better or worse, were to shape the nation's destiny in the years to come.

Chiang Kai Shek, a young army officer, was one of Sun's earliest supporters in the cause of a republic founded on both democratic and socialist principles. At that time he shared Sun's admiration for the way the Russian Bolsheviks had, in 1917, overthrown the Tsarist regime (which was similar in some ways to that of the Manchus). He went to Moscow, on Sun's behalf, to make friends with Lenin and the other new Soviet leaders. When Sun died, Chiang took control of the Kuomintang. But by then his politics had changed. He saw Communism as a threat to his own ambitions, especially after his marriage to Sung Mei Ling, the daughter of a millionaire businessman.

Mao Tse Tung was a hot-headed, rebellious lad, who ran away from home. He read widely and studied hard and got a job in the library at Peking University, where he learnt about Marxist politics. The old

Chiang Kai Shek, political head of China until he was overthrown by the Communists in 1949, when he fled to the island of Taiwan (Formosa).

imperial capital city, with its gorgeous palaces, also opened his eyes to the enormous gap between the privileged rich and the mass of poor people, including himself. 'I stayed in a little room with seven others,' he later recalled. 'When at night we were all packed fast on the *k'ang* [a type of heated stone floor] there was scarcely room for us to breathe. I had to warn people on each side of me when I wanted to turn over.' Mao, together with his close colleague and friend Chou En Lai, joined up with Sun, creating a Communist wing within the Kuomintang Party. They went on to set up Bolshevik-style soviets (workers' councils) in several provinces.

At the time of Sun's death, Chiang and Mao stood at opposite ends of the political spectrum.

Mao Tse Tung, founder of Chinese Communism, seen here as a young man in his home province of Hunan.

4 THE YEARS OF TURMOIL

The tender plant of Chinese democracy was soon uprooted. In 1927, Chiang formed a new Kuomintang government, based in Nanking, and became official Head of State. He also assumed the title of Generalissimo (military leader), and among his new edicts made membership of the Communist Party punishable by death.

The Communists, meanwhile, were gaining strong support, with their promises of land reform, among China's great mass of poor and downtrodden peasants. From their ranks, Mao and Chou had recruited and trained an army of nearly half a million men, a tough, well-disciplined force—the 'Red Army'. The stage was set for civil war.

Mao's Communist troops on the Long March—one of the most famous events in modern Chinese history.

The Long March

When Chiang launched his first attacks against the Communists, the troops of the new Red Army fought back with courage and skill. They employed the tactics of guerilla warfare. 'When the enemy advances, we retreat! When the enemy halts, we trouble them! When the enemy tries to avoid battle, we attack! When the enemy retreats, we pursue!' Chiang, however, had tanks, artillery and aircraft on his side, and gradually these assets began to tell. By 1934, Mao realized he must do something drastic to save the Red Army from ultimate destruction.

He planned to withdraw his forces into China's mountainous interior, where he hoped Chiang's forces could not reach them. This strategic retreat, known as The Long March, is perhaps the most famous event in modern Chinese history.

The Long March covered a distance of over 10,000 km (about 6,000 miles). Mao deliberately chose a route that took his army across some of China's wildest and most inhospitable country—through swamps, across tracts of near desert and over high mountain passes blocked by ice and snow. Sometimes, despite the route they followed, Chiang's aircraft and guns sought them out with bombs and shells.

Mao Tse Tung, photographed in a rare moment of relaxation during the period of the Long March.

A mass meeting of soldiers at the remote town of Yenan, at the end of the gruelling year-long March.

A veteran of the Long March recalled what it was like. 'As the days went by, there was less and less to eat. After our grain was finished we ate the horses, and then we lived on wild vegetables. When even the wild vegetables were finished, we ate our leather belts. After that we had to march on empty stomachs. One day we camped at the foot of a steep cliff. We were in such bad shape that we could not climb this cliff without first having something to eat. I collected some dry twigs to make a fire and started roasting my shoes. When they were cooked our squad leader cut them up into small bits and distributed these among the men to eat before climbing the cliff the next day.'

The Long March lasted a year. Of the 300,000 who started out, only about 20,000 survived. Their destination was the remote town of Yenan, in the northerly province of Shensi. There, far removed from Chiang's main centres of power, Mao slowly but surely rebuilt the Communist Party. One remarkable feature was the so-called 'Cave University', where thousands of political students lived and studied in the natural rock caves around Yenan.

Japan invades

Chiang might still have won the civil war, had it not been for the actions of Japan. China's eastern neighbour had for centuries been even more secretive and isolated than China itself. But, as we have seen, the Japanese had already come out of their isolation and proved themselves formidable opponents, both against China and Tsarist Russia.

In 1932 Japan invaded and occupied Manchuria, original homeland of the Manchu dynasty. The invaders reinstated the last surviving member of the dynasty as nominal ruler of their new territory of Manchukuo, though he took all his orders from the Japanese. In 1937, they extended their attack to the rest of China. Chiang called the Japanese invaders a 'cancer of the skin', whereas he said the Communists were 'a cancer of the heart'. He was, nevertheless, compelled to make a truce with Mao and the Communists in the face of the common enemy.

Japanese troops in China during their invasion of 1932. The threat from Japan forced opposing Chinese political parties to unite temporarily.

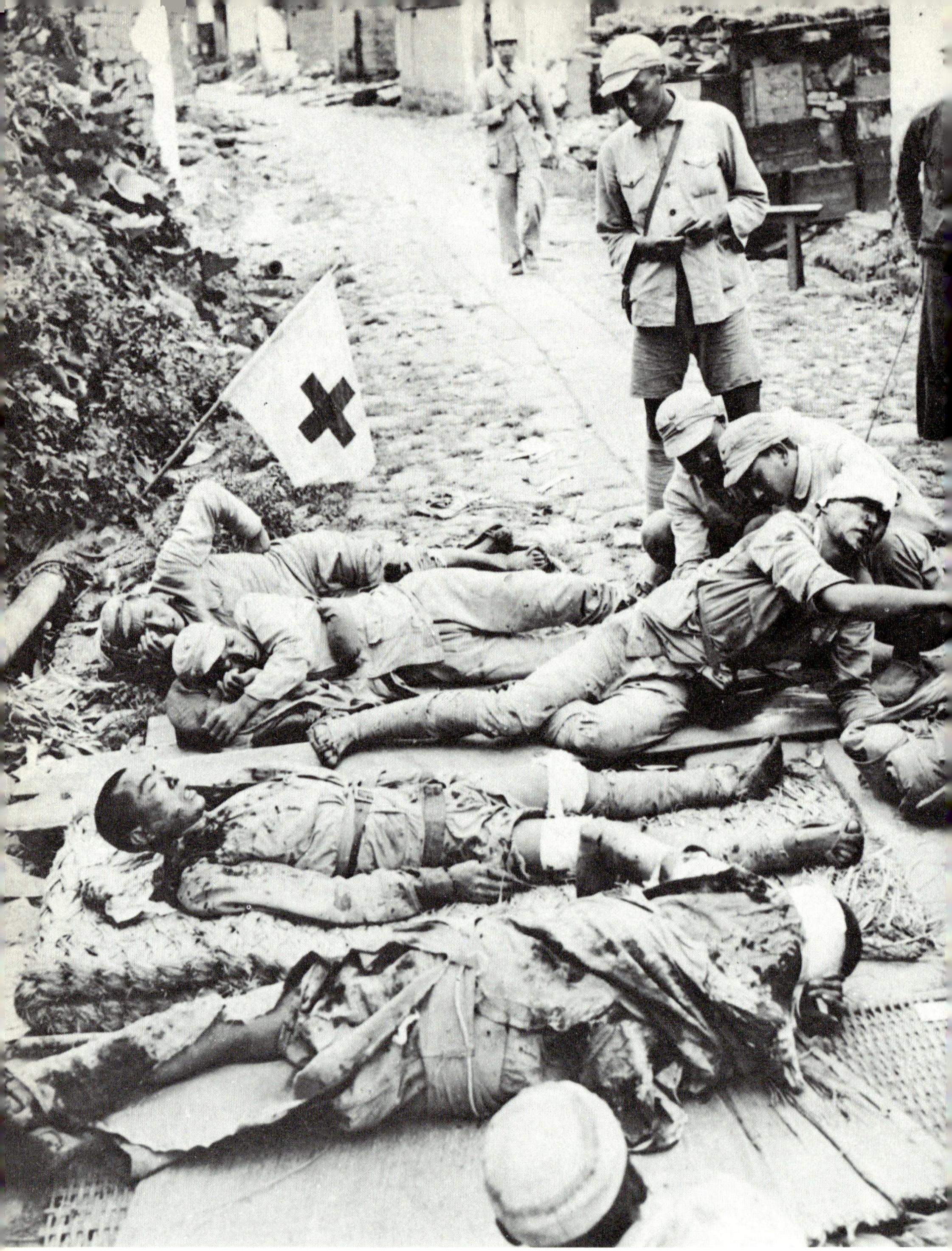

Badly-wounded Chinese troops at a makeshift first aid station during the Sino-Japanese war.

Chinese prisoners-of-war captured by the Japanese. The Japanese invasion brought suffering and hardship to many Chinese people.

Japanese forces captured many big towns and cities on or near the coast—Shanghai, Nanking, Hangchow—where their aircraft and warships could operate effectively. Inland, their armies met stiffer resistance, and their attack lost its momentum.

In those parts of the country occupied by the Japanese, the long-suffering Chinese peasantry and workers, though already used to every sort of hardship, experienced fresh horrors. At a coal mine in northern China, one old man remembered: 'We worked thirteen to sixteen hours a day. They whipped us every day. The Japanese imperialists did not treat the workers like human beings, but like animals. "Exchange coal with Chinese lives" was their slogan. When people became too ill to work they tied their legs and arms, carried them away and kicked them into a pit. No space was wasted in the hole; it was completely filled with bodies.'

Chiang Kai Shek, his wife Madame Chiang and General Joseph Stilwell smiled for the cameras, but there was little real trust between them.

The Second World War

On 7 December 1941, Japanese aircraft made a lightning strike against America's Pacific naval base at Pearl Harbour, in the Hawaiian Islands. This brought the United States into the Second World War, on the side of the British Commonwealth and the Soviet Union, against Nazi Germany, Italy and Japan. China, already fighting the Japanese, automatically joined the Allied cause.

The United States began to supply aid to China, and appointed General Joseph Stilwell to co-ordinate China's war effort. He had to deal with Chiang and the Nationalists. The two men smiled in front of the cameras, but there was little trust or goodwill between them. Stilwell, nicknamed 'Vinegar Joe' for his straight talking and sharp tongue, soon realized that Chiang was exploiting the situation for his own ends—promising much but doing little, waiting for the moment when he could turn on the Communists again. Stilwell also reported gloomily on the state of the Kuomintang and its fighting forces. 'The Chinese Red Cross is a racket. Stealing and sale of medicine is rampant. The army gets nothing. Malnutrition and sickness is ruining the army. The high-ups steal the soldiers' food. A pretty picture.' Many of the top posts were, indeed, held by Madame Chiang's relatives, who used the war for personal profit.

Soldiers of the Communists' new Red Army appearing before curious bystanders on the streets of Nanking.

The real beneficiaries of the war were Mao and the Communists. They mounted their own campaign against the Japanese, so gaining valuable experience as an efficient fighting force. Furthermore, when Japan surrendered to the Allies in August 1945, the Japanese soldiers still in China handed over nearly all their arms and other equipment to the Red Army (or People's Liberation Army). The Communists also took over the heavy industry that Japan had built up in Manchuria and the northern provinces. Their strength and morale were high.

5 THE PEOPLE'S REPUBLIC

To the world at large, Generalissimo Chiang Kai Shek remained China's legitimate leader and one of the victorious Allies, pictured with the US President Roosevelt, British Prime Minister Winston Churchill and the other Allied war leaders. And when the United Nations was founded in 1945, Nationalist China was given a place on the Security Council, alongside the United States, the Soviet Union, Britain and France. With so much public recognition abroad, Chiang had to win the battle at home.

Chiang Kai Shek, US President Roosevelt and Sir Winston Churchill, meeting in November 1943.

Chinese Communist troops carrying an assortment of weapons. Support for Chiang Kai Shek's Nationalists collapsed as the Communists advanced.

Mao triumphs

The Second World War was barely over when Chiang once again turned his Kuomintang army and air force against the Communists. Events, however, did not go as he expected. Not only were the Communists now much stronger, but the American General George Marshall, author of the Marshall Plan (the world-wide aid programme), stopped further aid to Nationalist China when he saw that it was being spent on war instead of peaceful reconstruction. This check to Chiang's plans was shortly followed by the Red Army's big counter-attack.

A Nationalist soldier and a small boy fleeing from Nanking.

From their bases in the north of the country, the Red Army swept southward, winning more converts and recruits as they went. In the words of one young man, 'When the Reds came to our village, everybody welcomed them. It was a happy time. Only the landlords ran. When the land was redistributed my parents received their share. So they were not sorry but very glad when I joined the "Poor People's Army".'

On the other hand, support for the Nationalists crumbled. Many of Chiang's own Kuomintang abandoned him. 'The number of defectors from the ranks of the Kuomintang increased by leaps and bounds,' wrote one observer. 'High officials and army officers freely offered their services to the advancing Red Army. It was the débâcle of a decaying system, in which for many, personal advantage was more important than duty.'

By April 1949, the Red Army had captured the Nationalist capital of Nanking and reached the great seaport of Shanghai, where thousands of desperate landowners, businessmen and other rich people were trying to flee the country. Chiang, with members of the Kuomintang and units of the armed forces still faithful to him, escaped to the neighbouring island of Formosa (Taiwan).

Students parading with banners in Shanghai to celebrate the Communist take-over in 1949.

Communist Party Chairman, Mao Tse Tung, proclaiming the creation of the People's Republic of China.

On 21 September 1949, Mao proclaimed the Chinese People's Republic. 'Our nation,' he said,' 'will never again be an insulted nation. The Chinese have stood up.'

The Constitution

Article One of the 1949 Common Programme or Provisional Constitution declared: 'The Chinese People's Republic is a state with a democratic people's dictatorship, led by the working classes, founded on unification of workers and peasants. It unites all democratic classes and different nationalities within the country.'

What this meant was made clearer in 1954, when elections were held for a National People's Congress to adopt a full constitution for

Mao with Chou En Lai, leaders of the new Communist government of China.

the new republic. This recognized four classes of citizen: working class (industrial workers), peasants (farm workers), petty bourgeoisie (shopkeepers and small traders), national bourgeoisie (professional people and managers). On the nation's new red flag, these categories of citizen were represented as four small stars grouped around a larger star symbolizing the Communist Party.

The 1954 Constitution provided for elections, progressing from village and provincial congresses (comparable to rural and county or borough councils) to a National People's Congress (a sort of parliament). The State Council (or Cabinet) carried out agreed policy through the various ministeries and commissions.

So, the 'democratic people's dictatorship' did allow for free elections, though these were almost entirely confined to voting for candidates as individuals rather than as representatives of different political parties. Some other parties besides the Communist Party were tolerated, but it was the latter that controlled affairs at all levels.

The new government, headed by Mao Tse Tung as chairman of the Communist Party and of the Republic, and Chou En Lai as the equivalent of prime minister and foreign minister, moved back from Nanking to the former imperial capital of Peking.

The first moves

One of the first acts of the new government was to honour the Party's pledge about land reform. Nothing was closer to the heart of the Chinese people than this. Exploitation of the peasants by cruel and greedy landowners had, for centuries, been one of the worst aspects of Chinese life. During the years of struggle, Mao had repeatedly promised to give land to the peasants. Now, across the nation, 100 million peasants and their families received plots of land from the State. Such a gesture won the trust of China's millions, while the government faced up to the far greater problem of how to transform Chinese society.

There was a darker side to the picture, as there inevitably is with major political upheavals. In the first weeks and months of the new republic, there was a nation-wide purge. People, in the countryside and in the towns, took their revenge on money-lenders, debt-collectors, and anybody else associated with the old days. Assaults and murders took place, as old scores were settled. The State also took part; members of the Kuomintang and other suspect citizens were rounded up, and their executions announced in advance over the radio or in the newspapers. In some places, public loudspeakers broadcast the sounds of the firing squads, so that the people could hear that rough justice was being administered. Mao himself later put the number of victims of such purges at around 750,000, but the total was probably a lot higher than that.

Agricultural reform was the highest priority of the new government. No longer privately-owned, land was divided between the people.

6 THE GREAT LEAP FORWARD

Until September 1949, China had been involved in war of one kind or another almost continuously for fifty years. Large areas of its cities were in ruins, industry was worn-out, fields were untended and millions were living in abject poverty. Such was the magnitude of the task of reorganization and reconstruction facing the new administration.

The Communist Government had two great assets. It could draw upon a huge work force of around 400 million (about half the total population), and it could count on the goodwill and support of the people. Mao used both to achieve what he called 'The Great Leap Forward'—the task of catching up economically with the other industrialized nations. There were to be some triumphs and some tragic mistakes along the way.

The Chinese people now faced the daunting task of rebuilding China's economy and industry.

'Blue ants'

Basing its policies on Soviet experience, the government took over large sections of industry and embarked on a series of Five Year Plans for the construction of bridges, roads and railways, power stations and dams, iron and steel plants, motor and tractor factories.

China's first motor vehicle production plant in 1957. It produced much-needed lorries, not private cars.

The Great Leap Forward meant endless hard work, but there was no shortage of labour. Here an army of workers is building a canal.

Women hauling heavy loads of stones. Spectators in the background have come from all over China to learn production techniques.

The Soviet Union supplied aid and teams of technical advisers. Even so, China was desperately short of basic industrial plant and equipment. So, the waiting millions were assembled. Dressed in standard blue labourer's overalls—men and women alike—they were recruited and mobilized like an army, and sent to work wherever they were needed. If there were no bulldozers or cranes available on a construction site, more of the 'blue ants' were called in. Here is one eye-witness account of the building of a dam: 'They swarm, cluster, split up again into strings, into little columns, finding their way around obstacles, coming to a halt at ditches and then hastily resuming their work. They are fetching white sand from all sides for the dam. Each one carries on his shoulder a bamboo pole with baskets slung from the ends . . .'

In the haste to get things going (people were even encouraged to build iron foundries in their back yards), equipment frequently broke down, precision tools were damaged by unskilled hands, or factories ground to a halt through power failures. Safety standards, too, were often overlooked. But always there was that huge fund of goodwill to overcome all difficulties and get on with the job.

Millions of factory workers, like these in a cotton mill, set themselves high production targets to further the aims of the revolution.

Gong Peihua was a young woman assigned the job of apprentice welder in a locomotive factory. 'I didn't like it at first,' she admitted. 'But my apprentice-master was very kind to me and I thought since I was young I ought not to be afraid of hardships. Little Chen, my colleague in our section, was much more vigorous in her work than I was, and the other workers never complained. So I thought, "Our factory is the only steam locomotive manufacturing plant in the whole country. When the locomotives leave the factory the *Datong Factory* plates have been welded by me". When I thought this, I felt quite proud of myself.'

Industrial production doubled in the first five years.

Collectivization

Unlike Stalin, the Soviet leader, who had given priority to heavy industry in the early days of the Soviet Union, Mao considered agriculture just as vital for China's future. Since time immemorial the country had faced periodic disasters caused by drought or flood. Such events, coupled with the reliance on rice as the staple food, meant starvation for millions. The Communists hoped to reverse the pattern of thousands of years with an agricultural policy as dynamic as that for industry.

The main thrust of the new policy was towards collectivization: teams

Workers on a collectivized farm tending the rice crop. Many new ideas, not all successful, were tried to increase agricultural output.

of farm workers ploughed, planted and harvested the crops, much as though they were working together on a factory production line. The scale of such operations varied; co-operatives were about the size of a traditional village and communes were new centres which employed thousands.

The Government also launched a 'war against nature'. It built huge reservoirs to irrigate dry land, and constructed dams across the Yangtze, Huang Ho and other big rivers, to control their flow and prevent flooding.

There were, at first, some spectacular increases in agricultural production. 'Eat until the skin of your belly is tight!' was the Government's confident slogan. But after a few years things started to go wrong. Directives about what to grow and how to grow it ignored local conditions and the experience of farmers on the spot. As one of them complained about the rice crop, 'Before, the water in the paddy used to be above the ankle. Now it's above the knee. But deep down the soil is no good. Too compact. It wasn't correct, but we couldn't help it. We got orders.' Big new reservoirs in previously dry regions also had an unexpected effect on local climatic conditions. And grazing land became very wet, but was found unsuitable for any other use.

There were some very bad harvests, and starvation threatened again. In agriculture the Government had tried to leap too far, and had to revise its plans. Collectivization was modified, farmers were encouraged once more to work the land in their own way, and as an added incentive were even allowed to sell some of their produce for private profit.

The Cultural Revolution

The Government wanted to change people's minds as fast as it was changing all other aspects of their lives. Mao at first said, 'Let a hundred flowers bloom,' meaning that everybody could learn from a free exchange of ideas. But soon the Government thought it saw signs of what it called 'decadent' or 'bourgeois' thinking, which were undermining the 'true' revolutionary spirit. It also accused some people of 'élitism', or intellectual snobbery, equally unacceptable in a true socialist society. So free speech began to be curtailed, a stronger propaganda line was adopted, and the nation embarked upon what was called The Cultural Revolution.

This was announced in 1966 in the Communist Party's official newspaper, *The People's Daily*. 'The great revolutionary waves will wash away all the filth of the bourgeois trends in art and literature. Something must be destroyed and something must be set up in the course of the Socialist Cultural Revolution. Without destruction there can be no construction.'

Above: Mao Tse Tung's portrait appeared everywhere and people began to think of him as a god.

Books of Mao's writings being sold to eager Chinese students at a college in Shanghai.

Red Guards parading through a Peking street in 1967, carrying portraits of Chairman Mao.

The Red Guards

The spearhead of the Cultural Revolution were the Red Guards – young men and women who were to purge the nation of all 'decadent', 'bourgeois' or 'imperialist' ideas and practices. They all had copies of a book called *The Thoughts of Chairman Mao*, known also as 'The Little Red Book', since it was bound in red, the symbolic colour of socialism. This was their Bible. The Red Guards wanted to change everything. Streets were re-named 'People's Road' or 'Anti-Imperialist Avenue'. Some groups tried to change the use of traffic lights, so that the red light meant 'go' instead of 'stop'!

'In our village,' said one former Red Guard, 'we knocked down statues of gods; ancestor tablets and things like that were burned. The main aim was to educate people to hand over or burn feudal paintings, books and religious objects. Some people did not agree and refused. Then the angry masses would put a paper hat on them, and a board on their shoulders [traditional marks of shame and disgrace], and parade them in the streets as "Capitalist-Roaders".'

Many young soldiers, like these, were Red Guards. During the Cultural Revolution some were driven to fanatical excesses.

A huge demonstration of support for Mao during the Cultural Revolution. Each man is holding a copy of Mao's famous 'Little Red Book'.

In the towns Red Guards stormed universities and schools, burning books they disapproved of, denouncing teachers, doctors, lawyers and any other 'intellectuals' whom they suspected of holding subversive views. Similar acts had been carried out in Nazi Germany.

The Government became thoroughly alarmed. The Red Guards were hastily disbanded. Many were drafted into the regular army to be disciplined, or sent to do the dirtiest work in factories or on farms. Once again, the authorities had tried to change things too quickly, and were forced to revise their thinking.

7 CHINA AND THE WORLD

In 1964, Red China made and tested its first atomic bomb. The Chinese Government then issued this warning: 'If the US imperialists are determined to launch a war of aggression against us, they are welcome to come sooner rather than later, to come as early as tomorrow. Let the British imperialists and the Japanese militarists come along with them. Let the modern revisionists act in co-ordination with them from the north. We will still win in the end!'

The People's Republic of China was born in the Cold War era—the period of rivalry and hostility between the two super powers, the United States and the Soviet Union, that stopped just short of all-out war. The new republic, as we shall see, was soon placed in a very unhappy position in the dangerous game of Cold War politics. At loggerheads with one superpower, it was alternately cold-shouldered and threatened by the other. It was this situation that inspired aggressive statements

Mao signing an agreement with the Russians in 1957. Two years later, relations between the two countries had broken down completely.

of the kind quoted above. These were largely bluster. China may have frightened others. But she was frightened too.

China and the Soviet Union

One of the new republic's first acts was to sign a treaty of Friendship, Alliance and Mutual Assistance with the Soviet Union. The latter, as we have seen, offered China aid and advice to help her build up her economy. The two largest Communist states—accounting for close on a third of the world's land area and population, and joined by a common frontier—thus presented a strong and united front.

Soon, though, cracks began to appear in this apparently rock-solid relationship. The Soviet leader, Joseph Stalin, argued that China should concentrate her efforts on heavy industry, as he had done in his own country. Mao considered agriculture to be equally important, and did not take kindly to outside pressure, from whatever source, as to how he should act. Then Stalin began to view a strong Red China not so much as an ally but as a future rival. There were already signs of open Sino–Soviet hostility by the time of Stalin's death, in 1953.

'Revisionism'

The new Soviet leadership, headed by Nikita Khrushchev, damaged relations with China for quite different reasons. Khrushchev, as leader of one of the two superpowers, was fearful of nuclear war, and anxious to reach some sort of accord or 'détente' with the United States. China, still full of revolutionary fervour, accused the Soviet Union of 'revisionism' (see the declaration quoted at the beginning of this chapter), that is, of betraying Marxist principles of world revolution, and of 'selling out' to the Americans. When, in 1959, Khrushchev met the US President Eisenhower for a summit conference, China angrily ordered all Soviet advisers out of the country. The Soviet Union retaliated by cutting off aid to China.

The Sino–Soviet quarrel then centred on their common frontier. China wanted the return of territories lost to Tsarist Russia (see page 17), and called the Soviet Union 'imperialists'. Both sides concentrated large numbers of troops at key areas along the border separating the two countries, particularly in the region of the Amur and Ussiri rivers marking the border with Chinese Manchuria. During the 1960s there were several outbreaks of fighting, before foreign ministers Chou En Lai and Andrei Gromyko agreed to call an end to hostilities.

China and the United States

America's Cold War policy was aimed at 'containing' the Communist world, by creating such military alliances as SEATO and NATO. With regard to the People's Republic of China, the United States would

Meetings between US President Eisenhower (left) and the Soviet leader Krushchev (right) angered the Chinese government.

In the 1950s, the Korean War brought China into open conflict with the United States.

not even recognize its existence, despite the fact that Britain and most other countries had done so. The US Government still insisted that Chiang Kai Shek and the Nationalists, now marooned on the island of Taiwan, represented the legitimate Chinese state, and they would have no dealings with the new Communist Government of 'Red' China. At one international gathering, the American Secretary of State, John Foster Dulles, refused to shake hands with Chou En Lai.

America's non-recognition of Red China did not stop the two nations lining up on opposite sides in several confrontations. Red Chinese and American armed forces first clashed during the Korean War of 1950–54, when China supported Communist North Korea against the American-backed South. Chinese and American forces were again in action against each other during the far longer and more costly Vietnam War of 1963–73.

The closest the two nations came to direct and open war was in 1954, when Red Chinese artillery shelled the small Nationalist-held off-shore island of Quemoy, as a prelude to invasion. Dulles, the chief architect of American containment policy, sent warships, armed with nuclear weapons, to the scene. It was a classic example of 'brinkmanship', of making warlike threats with seemingly serious intent, on the assumption that the other side would step back. In this case it worked. Mao called the Americans 'paper tigers', but with no nuclear weapons of their own at that date, it was the Chinese who backed down. Quemony, for the moment, remained in Nationalist hands.

'Ping-pong diplomacy'

The terrible Vietnam War brought about a sweeping change in American attitudes, especially towards Red China. Despite enormous American

Troops from US-backed South Vietnam set off on a mission against the Communist North Vietnamese.

An example of 'ping-pong diplomacy': US table tennis players on a Visit to Peking in 1970.

commitment in money and men, the Communists in Vietnam led by Ho Chi Minh, were winning. The United States Government was desperate to find a way out of the war without too much loss of face. They thought they saw such an opening in a *rapprochement*, or more friendly relationship, with the People's Republic.

The first steps in this direction took the curious form of table tennis matches between the two countries. In the absence of normal diplomatic relations, the teams were acting as unofficial diplomats, preparing the ground for future contact with some friendly sport. This 'Ping-pong diplomacy', as it was called, paved the way to a complete reversal of American policy. They wrote off Chiang and the Nationalists as a lost cause, and in 1971 accepted the People's Republic of China

The People's Republic of China was admitted to membership of the United Nations only in 1971.

President Nixon being greeted by Chairman Mao during his visit to China in 1972.

into the United Nations. The next year President Nixon visited China, and full diplomatic relations were established in due course.

China and the Third World

The large group of countries called the Third World are mostly Asian or African states that have gained their independence from old colonial powers such as Britain and France, and have remained outside the arena of Cold War politics. 'Non-aligned states' is another name for them, since they do not line up with either the Soviet Union or the United States in international affairs.

Because of its quarrels with both superpowers, the People's Republic of China soon saw itself as a natural leader of the Third World, speaking up for it against what China called 'the new imperialism' and 'great power chauvinism'. Chou En Lai and other Chinese leaders went on frequent tours to Pakistan, Sri Lanka, Zambia and other Third World nations. And as China's own economy grew, so it began to offer aid to these nations.

The only drawback in this much more successful area of China's foreign policy was the relationship with India, another leading Third World nation. The cause of the trouble was Tibet. This remote and land-locked state had traditionally been a part of China, and only gained a degree of independence in 1912, with the fall of the Manchu dynasty. Soon after the Communist victory of 1949, China reclaimed Tibet, sending in troops. Engineers were also sent in to construct a highway linking Tibet more securely with the rest of China. A revolt

Chou En Lai greets a Third World leader, the Prime Minister of Pakistan, on his arrival in Peking.

The Dalai Lama on his arrival in India after his expulsion from Tibet, following China's invasion of his country.

among Tibetan tribesmen led to China's expulsion of the Dalai Lama, Tibet's religious leader. He took refuge in neighbouring India. These events prompted India to arm its frontiers with China, and there were border clashes, similar to those involving the Soviet Union. Sino–Indian relations were severely strained.

A curious footnote to China's foreign affairs was its special relationship with the Communist state of Albania. Albania shared China's hatred of both American 'imperialism' and Soviet 'revisionism'. For a few years the giant nation of Asia and the tiny Balkan state formed an alliance of their own, though there was precious little that either country could do for the other.

8 CHINA TODAY

Mao Tse Tung and Chou En Lai, co-founders of the People's Republic of China, both died in 1976. Less than ten years later, a government spokesman said: 'We do not advocate the restoration of capitalism, yet we should not be overtly afraid of it. It is alright to have a bit of capitalism since it is not time to exterminate capitalism yet.' This appears to be an extremely cautious statement. A closer reading of it would suggest that, far from 'exterminating' it, the Government accepted capitalism as a fact of life. At all events, behind the statement lies another period of change, in attitudes and ideas, just as striking as anything that happened during the years of The Great Leap Forward and The Cultural Revolution.

The Gang of Four

Almost as soon as Mao and Chou were dead, an ideological struggle began in the higher ranks of the Chinese Communist Party. Mao's

The 'Gang of Four', who opposed the introduction of more moderate policies. Mao's widow, Chiang Ching, is on the right.

Portraits of Chairman Hua Feng replace those of the late Chairman Mao, and banners declare 'Death to the Gang of Four'.

widow, Chiang Ching, rallied those party bosses and government chiefs who wanted Marxist revolutionary policies to be maintained. She, and three other members of the existing politburo (the policy-making committee) who supported her, were labelled the Gang of Four. They were opposed by others in the Party and Government, who believed that the full-blooded revolutionary spirit had served its purpose in making the Republic strong, and that it was now time for a more moderate, even liberal period of government.

The moderates won the day, the Gang of Four were arrested, and Hua Kuo Feng became the new Party Chairman and Prime Minister.

Constitutional changes

Hua's administration brought in some important amendments to the 1954 Constitution.

'Citizens enjoy freedom to believe in religion and freedom not to believe in religion and to propagate atheism.' The Government made it clear by this that they were not backing religion, but they did allow people the right to make up their own minds on the matter. Buddhist temples and monasteries, Christian churches, Islamic mosques, closed since the time of the Cultural Revolution, opened their doors again, and there was fresh religious contact with people overseas.

'No citizen may be arrested except by a decision of a people's court, or with the sanction of a people's procurator.' The object of this amendment was to separate the law from politics (i.e. the Communist Party) and place it more firmly in the hands of the judiciary and the courts.

A sensational demonstration of the new legal code was the trial of the Gang of Four in 1981, on charges of crimes against the State. During the trial, Chiang Ching kept shouting quotations from her late husband's writings, and arguing about Marx and Lenin, though the judges ruled that they would not accept political arguments as evidence. The court was interested only in the defendants' actions, not in their political motives. Chiang Ching herself was found guilty and sentenced to death, though this was commuted to a term of imprisonment.

The wider significance of the trial was that, in the new political climate, even Mao's widow was not above the law. It served to clear the air of the 'Cult of Personality', or hero worship of Mao, that had reached such extremes during the Cultural Revolution.

A Communist Party communiqué issued soon after Mao's death had already agreed that, 'It would not be Marxist to demand that a revolutionary leader be free of all shortcomings and errors. It would also not conform to Comrade Mao's evaluation of himself. The Great Cultural Revolution should be viewed historically. The shortcomings and mistakes of the actual course of the revolution should be summed up at the appropriate time.' In other words, Mao was not a superman, and he made mistakes like anybody else.

Chiang Ching, Mao's widow, during her trial at the Supreme People's Court in Peking.

Today his memory is revered in China, but his actions and behaviour are open to criticism.

Welfare and education

Other new government decrees have had a greater impact on the lives of the mass of the Chinese people.

Birth control—an important issue in a country with the world's largest population—was discussed soon after the foundation of the People's Republic, and birth control programmes were introduced. Then, during the Cultural Revolution, they were halted again, on the grounds that if the Chinese population grew large enough, the nation would dominate the rest of the world by sheer weight of numbers!

A poster advising couples to have only one child, in an attempt to control the growth of the Chinese population.

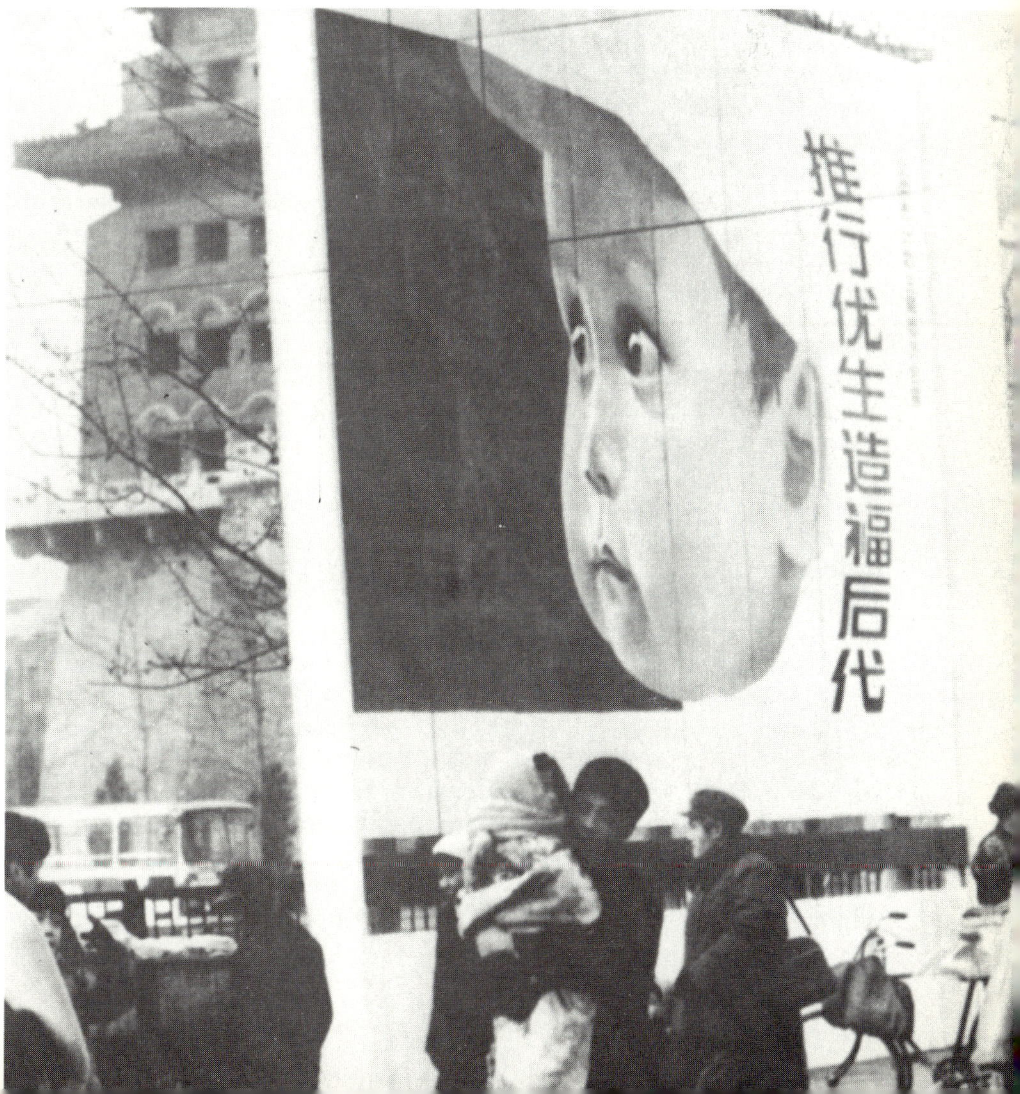

Reason finally prevailed. Today the Government rewards one-child families with welfare benefits, and penalizes those with more children. Other factors are helping. Community welfare has removed the old idea that a large family is some kind of insurance against poverty and old age. People are living longer, thanks to better medical care, but the birth-rate is currently falling, with the result that the population rise is slowing considerably.

Another quiet revolution is taking place today in the nation's classrooms. All over the huge country people speak different dialects of the Chinese language, sometimes finding it difficult or impossible to understand each other. Now every Chinese schoolchild learns Mandarin, the majority dialect of north China.

That is only half the linguistic problem that the Government is tackling. Written Chinese consists of thousands of individual symbols or ideograms, each standing for a particular object or idea. In times past, scholars prided themselves on their knowledge of these symbols, and on their skill at writing them down. Such a system, though, does not lend itself very well to modern science and technology. So the Government has adopted the Latin or Western alphabet as a way of spelling out Chinese words and making the whole language much more flexible and amenable to change. This *pin yin* system, as it is called, is as radical for China as if people in Europe and America had suddenly to learn to read and write in Chinese. It shows how open-minded today's Chinese leaders are prepared to be, to bring their nation into line with the rest of the modern world.

Great expectations

Teng Hsiao Ping, who succeeded Hua as China's leader, has said, 'Independence does not mean shutting the door on the world, nor does self-reliance mean blind opposition to everything foreign.' This is another carefully-guarded government statement, like the one quoted at the beginning of this chapter, that has turned out to mean far more than it actually says.

In 1980 China joined the World Bank and the International Monetary Fund. More recently still, the Chinese and British Governments settled the future of Hong Kong on the most friendly terms. The days of hostility between China and the rest of the world are well and truly over. Trade with other countries is growing by leaps and bounds.

China's most valuable exports are petroleum (much of this going to its former enemy and now major trading partner, Japan), textiles and clothing. In turn, China is buying expertise and sophisticated equipment, mainly from the United States and Western European countries, on nuclear and other advanced technologies.

But for the Chinese people as a whole, foreign trade means shops filling up with imported radios, television sets, cassette recorders,

Increasing contact with the West and Japan has introduced modern technology into China.

cameras. Foreign films are popular too, and, of course, pop music. The standard of living for the average Chinese citizen is still a long way behind that of most Western countries. A television set is still a highly-prized possession, a private car remains a dream. But the scene is set for a huge consumer boom, perhaps the world's biggest yet, taking account of China's population. Some Western vices, such as gambling, drugs and prostitution, are already in evidence. How to control these developments is a looming problem for a government still committed to the principles of socialist equality, planning and morality.

Meanwhile, the nation is again full of foreigners; not rapacious and unscrupulous merchants or invading armies any more, but tourists, come to see the Great Wall and other marvels of China's ancient past, and to admire what the nation, in the form of the People's Republic, has achieved in much more recent times.

A Western tourist with his Chinese guide. Tourists from the United States and Europe are becoming a familiar sight in many parts of China.

DATE CHART

1911 Fall of the Manchu dynasty and declaration of a Chinese Republic, with Sun Yat Sen as President.

1913 Yuan Shih Kai succeeds Sun as President. Imposes new dictatorship.

1916 Yuan assassinated. Period of anarchy and civil war.

1919 Mao Tse Tung founds the Chinese Communist Party.

1924 First National Congress. Sun re-appointed President of the Republic.

1925 Death of Sun. Leadership of Kuomintang Party and of the Republic passes to Chiang Kai Shek.

1927 Chiang forms new government and becomes official Head of State. New period of civil war between Chiang and the Communists.

1932 Japan invades and occupies Manchuria.

1934 The Long March—the Communist Red Army's strategic retreat.

1937 Japan invades the rest of China. Temporary pact agreed between Chiang and Mao.

1941 Japanese attack on Pearl Harbour. China enters Second World War on Allied side.

1945 Japan surrenders. Renewal of fighting between Chiang and the Communists. Nationalist China admitted to the United Nations.

1949 Communist victory over Chiang and the Nationalists. Proclamation of the Chinese People's Republic.

1950 Treaty of Friendship and Mutual Assistance with Soviet Union. The Republic enters the Korean War, and occupies Tibet.

1954 Full Constitution for the Republic. Communist shelling of Quemoy brings the Republic close to war with the United States.

1964 The Republic explodes its first atomic bomb.

1966–69 The Cultural Revolution.

1969 Border disputes with the Soviet Union and rupture of the Alliance.

1971 The People's Republic admitted to the United Nations.

1972 President Richard Nixon visits the Republic.
1975 Death of Chiang Kai Shek.
1976 Deaths of Mao Tse Tung and Chou En Lai. Hua Kuo Feng appointed Communist Party Chairman and Prime Minister.
1978 Amendments to the Constitution.
1981 Trial of the Gang of Four.
1982 Teng Hsiao Ping becomes the Republic's new leader.
1984 Agreement with Britain on the future of Hong Kong after expiry of the crown colony's lease in 1997.

FURTHER READING

General

Hookham, Hilda *A Short History of China* Longmans, 1969

Hsü, Immanuel *The Rise of Modern China* Oxford University Press, 1970

Zierer, Otto *History of China* Hamlyn, 1978

Documentary

Bonavia, David *The Great Cities: Peking* Time Life Books, 1978

Bonavia, David *The Chinese* Allen Lane, 1981

Clayre, Alasdair *The Heart of the Dragon* Collins, 1984

Inglis, Brian *The Opium War* Hodder and Stoughton, 1976

Short, Philip *The Dragon and the Bear: Inside China And Russia Today* Hodder and Stoughton, 1982

Tregear, T. R. *The Chinese: How They Live and Work* David and Charles, 1973

Warner, Marina *The Dragon Empress: Life and Times of Tzu Hsi* Weidenfeld and Nicolson, 1972

GLOSSARY

Bolshevik Member of the Russian Communist Party that seized power by revolution in 1917. Hence Bolshevism, or revolutionary Communism.

Bourgeoisie The middle classes, shopkeepers, clerks, teachers, and so on. In Communist societies 'bourgeois' is a term of abuse meaning reactionary or capitalist.

Capitalism Belief in private ownership and investment of wealth (capital), and the free operation of the laws of supply and demand.

Communism Political creed, based on Marxist doctrines (see below), about public ownership and redistribution of wealth ('from each according to his ability, to each according to his need').

Détente French word meaning 'relaxation', applied especially to the easing of tension between the two superpowers, the United States and the Soviet Union.

Dynasty A line of kings and queens from the same family, or similar ruling group.

Ideogram A sign or system used in some writing methods, including Chinese.

Ideology A body of political ideas.

Imperialism Empire-building.

Kuomintang Chinese Nationalist Party, the ruling party up to the founding of the People's Republic in 1949.

Lenin Real name Vladimir Ilyich Ulyanov. Leader of the Russian Bolshevik Revolution of 1917 and chief architect of the Union of Soviet Socialist Republics (USSR or Soviet Union).

Marxism Political doctrine based on the idea of a world-wide class struggle between those who create wealth (the workers or proletariat) and those who exploit it (capitalists). Named after the German philosopher Karl Marx.

NATO North Atlantic Treaty Organization. An international organization composed of the US, Canada, Iceland, Britain and 11 other European states, formed for the purpose of collective security.

Rapprochement A return to friendly relations between states after a period of crisis or tension.

Revisionism Communist term of abuse for modification of, or 'backsliding' on, Marxist principles.

SEATO South-East Asia Treaty Organization. Military alliance including the United States, Australia, New Zealand, Britain, France, and the Philippines.

Sino A prefix meaning Chinese. A sinologist, for example, is someone who studies China.

Socialism Sometimes used as another name for Communism (see above), but can be applied to more moderate left-wing political parties.

Soviet Russian word meaning 'council', especially workers' councils in communist countries.

Stalin Real name Joseph Dzhugashvili. Lenin's successor as leader of the Soviet Union.

United Nations International political organization, with headquarters in New York, founded in 1945 with the object of preventing war.

Note that, in Chinese, a person's surname comes first, and their 'first' names follow. Note also that there are different ways of transcribing Chinese names into English. A new system, based on *pin yin* (see page 68), gives the following spellings of some of the names and terms encountered in the text:

Conventional spelling	**New spelling**
Mao Tse Tung	Mao Zedong
Chou En Lai	Zhou Enlai
Hua Kuo Feng	Hua Guofeng
Teng Hsiao Ping	Deng Xiaoping
Peking	Beijing
Nanking	Nanjing
Kuomintang	Guomindang

Picture Acknowledgements

The illustrations were supplied by: BBC Hulton 4, 7, 10, 11, 12, 14, 15, 16, 17, 22, 24, 28; Camera Press 6, 9, 13, 21, 25, 34, 38, 41, 42, 44, 45, 49, 52, 56, 60, 64, 66; Sally and Richard Greenhill *front cover*, 70; John Hillelson Agency 26, 27, 33, 37, 58, 59, 62; Mansell Collection 18, 19; Peter Newark's Historical Pictures 20, 39; John Topham Picture Library 29, 30, 31, 32, 35, 36, 43, 47, 50, 51, 53, 55, 57, 61, 69, 69, Victoria and Albert Museum 8. The remaining pictures are from the Wayland Picture Library.

INDEX